I Can Make

MARVELOUS MOVERS

by Kristina A. Holzweiss
and Amy Barth

D0109832

Rookie
STAR™
Makerspace
Projects

SCHOLASTIC

TABLE OF CONTENTS

SPINNING TOP

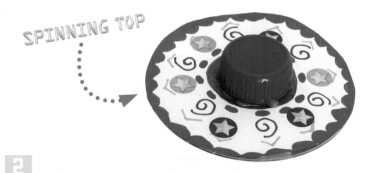

MOUNTAIN
CLIMBER

SNACKS

BALLOON CAR

ARE YOU A MAKER?

Makers are inventors, artists, and builders. In this book, you will learn how to make three marvelous movers: a spinning top, a mountain climber, and a balloon car.

These movers look very different from each other. But they have something in common—**motion**. Motion is when something moves.

Anyone can be a maker. You don't need fancy tools. You don't need to be a computer whiz. Are you creative and up for an adventure? Then you've got what it takes. Let's get started!

LLOON CAR

MOUNTAIN
CLIMBER

SPINNING TOP

MAKING CAN HAPPEN ANYWHERE!

You don't need a workshop to be a maker. You can make things in a classroom or on your kitchen floor. Project materials can be found around the house or at a craft shop.

You will need an adult's help with some steps. Like all inventors, you will try out your machines. Then you will change your designs to make them even better.

YOU CAN MAKE
A SPINNING TOP

The spinning top is one of the oldest toys in the world. The way it works is pretty simple. You just give it a twist and send it spinning. The secret to a top's motion is in its shape.

You can make your own spinning top and see how long it will whirl!

HOW A SPINNING TOP WORKS

SHOULDER
This part is much wider than the point. That shape keeps the top from falling over.

CROWN
Grab the crown and twist it hard. This will send the top spinning.

POINT
The spinning top balances on its point.

BODY
The body's acorn shape helps the top spin longer.

A spinning top works best on a smooth surface. That is because there is very little **friction** between the surface and the top. Friction causes the top to slow down.

A top will stop spinning eventually. But you can find design tricks to help your top spin for a long time.

FRICTION

Friction is created when two objects rub against each other. The **force** acts in the opposite direction to the way an object wants to travel.

Think about what happens if you run down the sidewalk and stop quickly. The friction between your shoes and the cement is what helps slow you down.

INSTRUCTIONS

- ☐ CD
- ☐ Paper
- ☐ Pencil
- ☐ Scissors
- ☐ Markers, crayons, colored pencils, stickers
- ☐ Regular glue stick
- ☐ Hot glue gun
- ☐ Hot glue sticks
- ☐ Plastic bottle cap
- ☐ Marble

1 Lay the CD on the paper. Trace around the outside with a pencil. Cut out the circle. (Be careful to cut on the line.)

2 Decorate the paper circle. Be as creative as possible!

e the glue stick to ach the circle to top of the CD.

Ask an adult for help using the hot glue gun. Attach the bottle cap to the center of the circle. This will be the crown, or handle, of your top.

Turn the CD over. Ask an adult for help using the hot glue gun. Attach the marble to the center of the CD. This will be the point of your top.

MAKE IT MOVE

Place your spinning top on a flat surface. Make sure it is resting on the marble. Twist the cap to make the top spin.

TEST IT

Test your top on a wood or tile floor. Time how long it spins. Write down the number of seconds. Now try spinning your top on a carpet. On which surface did your top spin the longest? Why do you think that is?

CHANGE IT

····▶ Instead of the CD, try using a paper plate or a jar cap. What material works best?

····▶ Tape pennies to the top to make it heavier. Does the top work better when it is lighter or heavier?

Surface	Spin Time
Tile Floor	
Carpet	

YOU CAN MAKE
A MOUNTAIN CLIMBER

Climbers explore some of the tallest mountains in the world. They hold on tight so they don't fall off! If a climber falls, he or she could crash to the ground. Luckily, mountain climbers are attached to ropes. The ropes catch them if they fall.

You can make your own mountain climber and help it climb high!

HOW A CLIMBER ASCENDS

The force of the climber pulling his body up is greater than the force pulling it down.

STRENGTH

GRAVITY

Gravity is a force that pulls things to Earth.

ROPES

Ropes stop the climber if he falls.

Two forces are at work in this project. The force of your hands pulling the strings is greater than the gravity pulling the climber toward the ground. Once the project is finished you will see that the harder you pull the strings, the faster the climber will move up. One force is proportional to the other.

DISCOVER MORE ABOUT

FORCE

Force is the push or pull on an object. Gravity is a natural force. It pulls things down toward the earth. The heavier an object is, the stronger the gravity that pulls it toward the earth. When you push or pull something you are using force, too.

INSTRUCTIONS

- ☐ Pencil
- ☐ Poster board
- ☐ Scissors
- ☐ Markers, crayons, colored pencils, yarn, googly eyes
- ☐ Ruler
- ☐ Straight plastic drinking straw
- ☐ Clear tape
- ☐ Penny
- ☐ 4 feet of yarn
- ☐ Two plastic pony beads

1

Draw a mountain climber on the poster board. It should be a little bigger than your hand. Cut out the climber and decorate it.

2

Measure and mar┃ two 2-inch pieces ┃ the straw. Cut the┃ from the straw.

MAKE IT MOVE

Pull the yarn above the mountain climber's head. Twist it once to create a loop. Then hang the climber on a doorknob. Hold one end of the yarn in each hand. Pull the ends apart to make the climber go up. Bring the ends together to make it come down.

ce the climber
h the decorated
e down. Place the
w pieces on the
ber. They should
next to each
er, about 1 inch
ve the legs.
e them down.

Tape the penny
below the straws,
just above the
climber's legs.

Thread a piece of
yarn up through the
bottom of the straw
on the left. Thread
it down through
the top of the straw
on the right. Slide
a pony bead onto
each end of the
yarn. Knot each
end of the yarn.

TEST IT

How hard do you need to pull the yarn to make the mountain climber rise as high as possible?

CHANGE IT

····► Change the positions of the straws. Does it change how hard you have to pull on the yarn?

····► Tape one or two more pennies onto your climber. Does that make it harder to pull the climber up? Why do you think that is?

YOU CAN MAKE

A BALLOON CAR

A real car is powered by an engine. The engine turns the axle. That is a long rod that connects the wheels to the car's body. The axle makes the wheels spin. That makes the car move.

Buses, bikes, wagons, and motorcycles all have wheels and axles. You can build a car that moves using wheels and axles, too!

HOW A CAR WORKS

ENGINE
The engine is the heart o
the car. It helps give the
car power so it can drive

WHEELS
Wheels are round.
Circles roll more
easily than shapes
with sharp angles.

AXLE
The axle is a rod that
connects wheels.

Your toy car will be powered by the air in a balloon. When you blow up the balloon, it fills with air. When you let go of the balloon, the air quickly escapes. The **energy** from the movement of the air pushes the car forward.

You can make a balloon car—and test the limits of how far it can travel.

DISCOVER MORE ABOUT
ENERGY

Energy allows things to change, grow, and move. People and animals get energy from food. Light bulbs get energy from electricity. Without energy, there would be no life or motion on Earth.

INSTRUCTIONS

1

Cut the cardboard into a cool car shape. Decorate the car and place it to the side.

2

Ask an adult for h[elp] making the wheels Use the screwdriv[er] to poke a hole through the center of each bottle cap

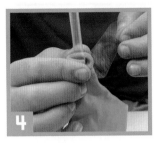

4

5

.h the dowels into
 of the straws.
 se are your axles.
 .h the wheels onto
 ends of the axles.
 ce the car
 corated side down.
 .e the middle of
 axle to the front
 of the car. Tape
 middle of the
 .er axle to the
 ck end of the car.
 the car over.

Now make the car's
engine. Place the
tip of the remaining
straw into the
balloon. Use tape to
attach the balloon
to the straw. Make
sure it is sealed.

Tape the straw and
balloon to the car.
Make sure some of
the straw is sticking
out of the back of
the car.

MAKE IT MOVE

Blow up the balloon
through the straw and
then pinch the end closed.
Place the car on a smooth
surface, release the straw,
and watch it go!

TEST IT

Try out your car on a wood or tile floor. How far does it move once you let go of the balloon? Test out your car on other surfaces, like a carpet or grass. On which surface did your car travel the farthest?

CHANGE IT

····▶ Add more balloons or wheels to your car. Does it go faster?

····▶ Change the size of the wheels by using CDs or paper plates instead of bottle caps.

····▶ Make the car's body out of a water bottle, soda can, or egg carton instead of cardboard.

MASTERS
OF MOTION

LEONARDO DA VINCI

Leonardo da Vinci is a famous artist. He was also an inventor. In 1478 he drew pictures of a cart that moved on its own. The picture reminds people of a car. The first car wasn't invented until the 1880s—more than 400 years after Leonardo's drawings.

ISAAC NEWTON

More than 300 years ago, scientist Isaac Newton discovered gravity. This force is what pulls objects toward the Earth. Some people say the idea of gravity came to Newton when an apple fell out of a tree onto his head!

HENRY FORD

The first gas-powered cars were invented in the 1880s. Lots of people wanted cars. Each car took a long time to build, and they were too expensive. Henry Ford figured out how to build cars more quickly and cheaper.

ALICE RAMSEY

In 1909, Alice Ramsey became the first woman to drive across the United States. She was 22 years old. The drive was 3,800 miles (6,116 kilometers). It took her 59 days. Today's cars are much faster. That same trip now takes just four days!

EDMUND HILLARY
TENZING NORGAY

STEFANO MASO

Edmund Hillary of New Zealand and Tenzing Norgay of Nepal were the first people to climb to the top of Mount Everest, the world's highest mountain. Hillary and Norgay made the tough journey in 1953.

In 2015, Italian breakdancer Stefano Maso broke the World Record for the most head spins in a row: a whopping 49 times without stopping! Only Maso's head and hands were allowed to touch the floor.

TIMELINE:
MACHINES THAT MOVE

Check out this timeline about some of the coolest movers ever made.

3200 BCE
Wheels are invented.

1868 CE
The first wristwatch is made in Hungary.

1884
The first roller coaster opens in America in Coney Island, New York. It goes about six miles per hour and costs a nickel to ride.

1885
The first automobile is built, probably by Karl Friedrich Benz.

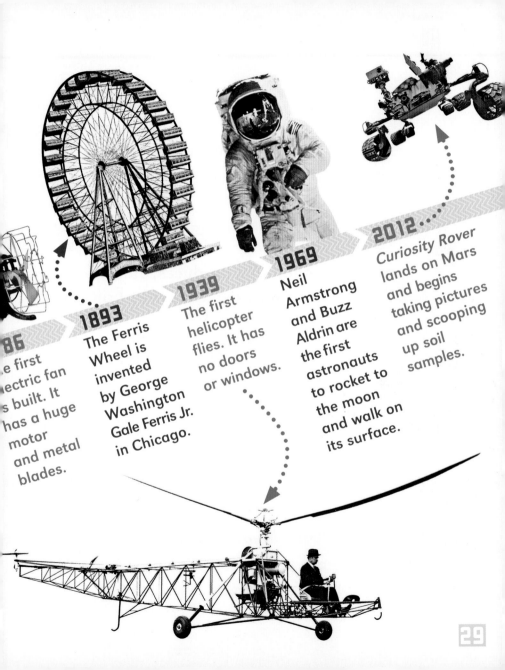

1886
The first electric fan is built. It has a huge motor and metal blades.

1893
The Ferris Wheel is invented by George Washington Gale Ferris Jr. in Chicago.

1939
The first helicopter flies. It has no doors or windows.

1969
Neil Armstrong and Buzz Aldrin are the first astronauts to rocket to the moon and walk on its surface.

2012
Curiosity Rover lands on Mars and begins taking pictures and scooping up soil samples.

Energy *(en-ur-jee)*

Power from coal, electricity, or other sources that makes machines work.

Force *(fors)*

Any action that produces, stops, or changes the shape or the movement of an object.

Friction *(frik-shuhn)*

The force that slows down objects when they rub against each other.

Motion *(moh-shuhn)*

The act or process of moving or the way something moves.

ABOUT THE AUTHORS

Kristina A. Holzweiss was selected by School Library Journal as the School Librarian of the Year in 2015. She is the founder of SLIME—Students of Long Island Maker Expo and the President of Long Island LEADS, a nonprofit organization to promote STEAM education and the maker movement. In her free time, Kristina enjoys making memories with her husband, Mike, and their three children, Tyler, Riley, and Lexy.

Amy Barth is a writer and editor specializing in science content for kids in elementary through high school. She writes about robots, penguins, volcanoes, and beyond! She lives in Los Angeles, California.

Scholastic Library Publishing wants to especially thank Kristina A. Holzweiss, Bay Shore Middle School, and all the kids who worked as models in these books for their time and generosity.

Library of Congress Cataloging-in-Publication Data

Names: Holzweiss, Kristina A., author. | Barth, Amy, 1984- author.
Title: I Can Make Marvelous Movers/by Kristina A. Holzweiss and Amy Barth.
Description: New York, NY: Children's Press, An Imprint of Scholastic Inc.,
[2017] | Series: Rookie star makerspace projects | Includes bibliographical
references and index.
Identifiers: LCCN 2016051666 | ISBN 9780531234136 (library binding: alk. paper) | ISBN
9780531238820 (pbk.: alk. paper)
Subjects: LCSH: Science—Experiments—Juvenile literature. | Inventions—Juvenile literature. |
Handicraft—Juvenile literature.
Classification: LCC Q164 .H74 2017 | DDC 507.8—dc23
LC record available at https://lccn.loc.gov/2016051666

APR 2 4 2019

Design: Judith Christ-Lafond & Anna Tunick Tabachnik
Text: Kristina A. Holzweiss & Amy Barth
© 2018 Scholastic Inc.

All rights reserved. Published in 2018 by Children's Press, an imprint of Scholastic Inc.
Printed in China 62
SCHOLASTIC, CHILDREN'S PRESS and associated logos are trademarks and/or
registered trademarks of Scholastic Inc., 557 Broadway, New York, NY 10012.

1 2 3 4 5 6 7 8 9 10 R 27 26 25 24 23 22 21 20 19 18

Photos ©: 6 scissors: fotomy/iStockphoto; 6 crayons: Charles Brutlag/Dreamstime; 6 tape: Carolyn Franks/Dreamstime; 6 glue gun: Nilsz/
Dreamstime; 6 markers: Floortje/Getty Images; 6 straws: Olga Dubravina/Shutterstock; 6 marble: David Arky/Getty Images; 6 CD: Ro-
man Sigaev/Shutterstock; 6 bottle cap: Mrs_ya/Shutterstock; 6 pencil: antomanio/iStockphoto; 8 top: philipimage/Can Stock Photo, Inc.;
8 acorns: strawberrytiger/Shutterstock; 9 shoes: Humbak/Alamy ImagesAlamy Images; 9 background and throughout: Hughstoneian/
Dreamstime; 10 left and throughout: somchaij/Shutterstock; 12 top right: TPopova/iStockphoto; 12 top left: AnatolyM/iStockphoto; 12
bottom right and throughout: FineArtCraig/iStockphoto; 14: Serge Tabachnik; 15 center: BLOOM image/Getty Images; 18 bottom left:
GooDween123/Shutterstock; 18 bottom center: Carolyn Franks/Dreamstime; 20: weicheltfilm/iStockphoto; 21 bulb: Francesco Perre/
EyeEm/Getty Images; 24 bottom: Chones/Shutterstock; 25 top left: Culture Club/Getty Images; 25 bottom left: Veneranda Biblioteca
Ambrosiana/DEA/Getty Images; 25 bottom right: SHEILA TERRY/SCIENCE PHOTO LIBRARY/Getty Images; 25 top right: Anton Ignatenco/
Dreamstime; 26 bottom right: Detroit Public Library; 26 bottom left: Ed Vebell/Getty Images; 26 top left: Library of Congress; 26 top
right: Bain News Service/Library of Congress; 27 right: Warrengoldswain/Dreamstime; 27 left: The Granger Collection; 28 left: Dmitriy
Margolin/Getty Images; 28 center: Sarin Images/The Granger Collection; 28 top right: Bettmann/Getty Images; 28 bottom right: Watch
with wristband, ca 1910, gold and diamonds, Goldsmith art, 20th century/De Agostini Picture Library/A. Dagli Orti/Bridgeman Art
Library; 29 left: DEA/A. DAGLI ORTI/Getty Images; 29 top center left: North Wind Picture Archives/Alamy Images; 29 center right:
SSPL/Getty Images; 29 right: JPL-Caltech/MSSS/NASA; 29 bottom: Popperfoto/Getty Images; 30 top: Francesco Perre/EyeEm/Getty Images; 30 center top: BLOOM image/Getty Images; 30 center bottom: Humbak/Alamy Images.

All instructional images by Jennifer A. Uihlein.
All other images by Bianca Alexis Photography.